PURL

PURL

JO DIXON

To Elizabeth,
With love
from Jo
28/07/2020

Shoestring Press

Printed by imprintdigital
Upton Pyne, Exeter
www.digital.imprint.co.uk

Typesetting and cover design by narrator
www.narrator.me.uk
info@narrator.me.uk
033 022 300 39

Published by Shoestring Press
19 Devonshire Avenue, Beeston, Nottingham, NG9 1BS
(0115) 925 1827
www.shoestringpress.co.uk

First published 2020
© Copyright: Jo Dixon
© Cover image: Jo Dixon

The moral right of the author has been asserted.

ISBN 978-1-912524-71-6

ACKNOWLEDGEMENTS

I am grateful to the editors of the following anthologies and journals in which several of these poems first appeared, sometimes in different versions: *Flakes of a Fire: Writing East Midlands Winners' Anthology* (2016), *Furies: A Poetry Anthology of Women Warriors* (For Books' Sake, 2014), *In Transit: Poems About Travel* (The Emma Press, 2018); *New Walk* (Issue 8, Spring/Summer, 2014), *Our Beating Heart: NHS70* (erbacce-press, 2018), *South Bank Poetry* (November 2018), *Species* (Launderette Books, 2012), *The Interpreter's House* (Issue 56, 2014), The Poetry School Online, *Twenty-Five* (Shoestring Press, 2019), *Women's Writing in the Midlands, 1750–1850: Susanna Watts and Elizabeth Heyrick, A Poetry Collection* and *Writing Lives Together* (The Centre for New Writing, University of Leicester, 2017).

Thanks also to William Palmer and Melos Press who published some of these poems in the pamphlet, *A Woman in the Queue* (2016).

I am also grateful to the Arts and Humanities Research Council and Midlands4Cities DTP for their support.

Special thanks are due to my family, friends and colleagues, in particular Jeremy and Jacob, Jacquie and Keith Quinton, Sarah Jackson, Rory Waterman, Becky Cullen, Lynda Clark and John Lucas.

CONTENTS

III (v. colloquial) *to turn upside down, overturn, capsize, to pitch or tumble head over heels*

I

(n.) gold or silver wire thread used for bordering and embroidering

THE ARDABIL CARPET

Expecting the downlighters
that bleed each wool-knot
on the hour on the half-hour
I nudge the barrier with my shins

and lay the shape of my breath
on the display case where flowers
tinted with pomegranate-rind
will lose another shade.

The tang of *Bisto* blends
with one more cigarette
glowing in the ashtray
and I play house on the carpet

in the front-room where Grandma
still tied into a money apron
scored with potato-soil
warms and waits for the Sunday roast.

PROVENCE

Arthur raises her on one hand, exciting muscles
moulded by Fleet Street paper reels. Below
crayon daisies cluster on sheets lifted
from his nightshift. Lil clicks her dentures.

And the girl nests in his paunch while he spins
the tale about his finger, shot away in the war.
She presses the bone ledge beneath his beaten skin;
Lil sips water from a rose-brimmed teacup.

When his heart's had enough of blotting vodka
out of the carpet and gathering porcelain shards,
she's on a train to Aix, picking at a ham sandwich
in the corridor, hairpinned legs flattening her chest.

At Sabine's house she tastes *ratatouille* and a nip
of *pastis*, buys *calissons* and watches milk-white
horses occupy the Camargue. Then she comes home
wearing turquoise earrings and her first proper kiss.

OVERTURE

A young stag all emerging antlers
raises his nose toward a teenage couple

over by the cedar stump shrugging off its bark,
exposing bouclé ridges, silky crevices
and fibrous escarpments gripped by webs.

On the next bench
moisture in wooden slats soaks their jeans
and a plaque reassures *Pleasure and Companionship*
                              Found Here
while he defines her shoulder blade with his fingertips

and toes the browned pine needles pulped in the mud
like wedding rice on a wet day
                    If you want to be in a relationship—

Later he steers her around the Camellia House
rainwater performing on glazed roof-lights
and petals warping on stone flags

her eyes downcast, tracing the entangled circles of bronze grilles
above heating ducts where pennies have been lost.

HOLIDAY BALLROOM

Cherry Blossom black shine
on his toes
Mr Sheen—a slick glide
on his soles
her hair   set to wave
and pleats in feather-flares
                            just
                            above her knee

cross-legged socks and sherbet edge
the floor; follow her diamante t-bars

and he wants the trophy
and she wants to dance

PIECEWORK

Alongside the portable radio
slung from his coat peg

he slips her ballet shoe
inside out over the last

layers burlap, hessian
and flour-paste glue

fashions blocks to inflame
her joints, tear at her tendons.

Wax thread joins upper to sole
and shavings curl on the concrete

as he teases and clips
with pliers that sculpt

the contours of her feet.
In the shank he presses his emblem: ♣

Overnight the oven sets her blocks,
roasts the grain-weevils burrowed

inside, and by lunch next day a dab
of washing-up liquid has erased

his finger-marks, restored
her peach satin unbruised.

LEADING LADY

The reel-box on the floor
insists KODAK CAPTIVATES EVERYONE.
I look up, drawing breath
and when the gummy film
starts to feed from spool
to spool particles of dust
and skin flare in the projector's beam.
I follow them into the hiss
and flicker of the screen.

    A man behind his rose-bush hedge
     stops the mower each time she sulks past,
    eyes down on the pristine Clarks.
    An empty satchel knocks against her hip,
    grey pleats kick out from each knee.

My Dad choreographed that rehearsal;
the buses only gave him Sundays off back then.

    Bunting clacks over paste-tables butted end to end,
    over chairs—plastic, mahogany, teak—over the girl
    in a gingham school-dress, draped
    with two Union Jack tea towels
    tacked at the shoulders, nipped in by a belt.

Dad fetched me that stool from our front-room bar
and those glacé cherries I'm dipping in my Babycham.

    'Tell us your name and who you are!'
    Pink crepe-paper sleeves itch
    the crook of her elbow as the mesh
    of a microphone brushes her lips.
    In the line-up by the pool

she picks at the edges of heart-
shaped stickers on her skirt.
July rain bleeds the pink.

The year after Mum dressed me up as a bunny girl,
the one after that I was Queen Elizabeth I.

THE NEIGHBOUR'S SHOES

We were goin' on a friend's boat, then she refused. They thought bad of her. She put up with a lot, hid the pain. Take the shoes. You're a schoolteacher, you must be able to find some use. Three pairs push for space in the carrier: grey, black, navy. *She never knew what she wanted t'wear. Come up and see for yoursen.* In the box-room he's laid out her clothes. By the pillow dresses, then trousers, jumpers, blouses … *Good stuff she hardly wore, what about this?* I hold the cardigan up under my chin to show him it's too big. *My daughter won't go through it.*

At the bottom of the stairs he talks half an hour more. *I'm going home to Scotland, my son says no, but I've bought a new car.* He'd been in Aden. *Brigade's best sharpshooter*—I've heard the stories before. They could be true. *I was goin' home 40 year ago; she kept me here* and I touch his arm. *You'd better get back to the littl'un. Don't forget your shoes.*

ON READING *SOME MEMORIALS FOR THREE GENERATIONS OF A FAMILY*

Indigo letters have bled through
from below, interrupting the sentences
in this typescript of Grandma's journal:

translucent sheets of foolscap
keyed on a metallic-blue Imperial
while I country danced at school.

Now each page-flick loosens skin flakes
from Mum's fingers and green treasury tags
hook in the punched holes.

A sallow sheet rips at the margin,
falls from the manila folder on her lap,
settles beside her plaid slippers

and we pause to eat sandwiches from a tray.
Ruptured blood vessels are fanning out from her wrist.

BRIDGE SLIDE / 'AND THE PHOENIX HAS COME'*

Jacking lifting resetting dropping pushing forward; sliding the steel warren truss *slowly across the dusty sky* in nightly cycles of 2.6m. *Its voice*—welded tubular—*dangles glittering in the soft valley* of the station: a showpiece overbridge on Victorian pier foundations. *Its feathers shake from the eye* with an upper chord described by a circular arc; *its ashes smoke from the breath* in a study of heritage and aesthetics—*flaming and dripping flame.* Iron caissons drive into platform granite slab, *tremble the altar of its death and its birth; where it descends where it offers itself up and naked the newborn* in April *crows in the blaze,* 'The crossing is back'.

* This collage poem is assembled from an article in the New Civil Engineer about the bridge construction over Nottingham Station as part of the Tram works *(New Civil Engineer,* 28/02/13, pp. 14–15) and Ted Hughes' poem, 'And the Phoenix has Come', from *Moortown* in *Ted Hughes: Selected Poems (1957–1981),* (1982, London: Faber and Faber, 1988), p. 209.

HAIDA CHIEF

One undivided
red cedar trunk,
carved softly:

Frog is closest
to the ground,
his tongue lolls;

Bear splays his nostrils
up at Raven who drags
the clouds down with his beak;

at the top Thunderbird,
displays his tufted head,
surveys the ocean—

his ovoid-eyes
blackened with magnetite,
mouth tinted hematite-red.

So, what is your family's founding myth?
The story that passes between generations?

I draw a finger along the cracks where the cedar
breathes and contracts in a different place each day until
life-giving rain, snow, sun return it to the earth.

Frog's contours press into my back;
Raven prises open the clamshell giving birth to your line.
See how he's releasing the sun from its box?

When I follow Hummingbird to the places where you hunt
and fish and sprinkle eagle-down on the floor to welcome
important guests, Thunderbird beats his wings
                                    and the storm comes.

A SHOWING

after Raphael Hefti

I – Forest

I am

between metal tubes
propped in cavities
of a gallery-roof.

Each slanting trunk is
renewed by electrical heat
at different degrees:
striae of kingfisher-blue,
silver, marigold.

I thread

between trunks
displace
one step
with another.

II – *Witch Powder*

He revels in the basement:
scatters moss-spores
over giant sheets
of *Fuji* high-gloss
taped to the floor,
ingests the Lycopodium
thinning his hair

and as the dust spreads
he ignites the oxygen
surrounding its particles

and fixes a moment
he can't quite control:
pink coral or the cosmos

DIAPAUSE

The water was too hot:
sud-soaked cuffs and hands
(suddenly puce) from the washing up

then a jive
in my far peripheral

against the window, inside
the bowed side of our small-car garage
with blistered doors and textured glass.

The left-hand door scraped
over concrete and knapweed until
it opened just enough for me to squeeze in
   next to six bin bags
    of baby clothes, a paddling pool,
    and a family tent with headroom.

In the fanlight a small caramel and jet
tortoiseshell was vibrating the muscles
in its thorax, preparing its wings

like the butterfly blotted with poster paint
onto one half of the bleached sugar-paper
(folded over, smoothed out, then opened out)
slipping down our fridge.

The years had jammed the window shut,
so, with the lid of a jigsaw puzzle I teased
it along the sill, the wall, the doorpost.

The day after, another. The day after, another

IT'S FLO'S LAST DAY AT THE SHOP

at home with her patchwork of fruit and veg.
Cotton vest under blouse under cardy under
coat—but open all year, to the weather that edges
inside her eggshell bones. When the school boys
fall in for the six o'clock harvest of lost pennies,
she is reading her hands, sculpted by root and coin
with nails polished in dirt.

Next day she's up early, behind her nets,
looking across the street at a girl zipped in Thermalite
who tugs at the shutters, bounces her ponytail.
A moth plays staccato inside the floral drum shade.
Tassels flutter. She unseats it with a scoop
then rubs its soil-coloured scales into her palm.

MOVING HER ON

So her sons
manoeuvre the easy chair
and retrieve her binoculars from the hollow.

They shuffle the sideboard, its top-drawer
lined with tissue-wrapped thimbles,
to the back of a white Bedford.

When it's all packed up
she rides in the cab between them;
her wedding cutlery rattles behind.

A mile from home
the van's headlights catch a tawny owl
falling.

And later it waits
on a fence post girdled by pellets
opposite her black window.

If she were there
tucking a stray hair behind her ear,
setting down the binoculars, rising to give in to bed

he'd bob and weave his head,
flap silently out of sight.

UBUNTU

'You can't be human all by yourself', Desmond Tutu

In praise of Sister Jerome reading to boarders under the
Casuarina growing quickly: a windbreak of grey-green weeping
branchlets, yellow spikes, seeding couples with ruddled heads,
cones displayed on her desk at the front. In praise of Mr Kondolo
sprucing up his shoes on the crease-line of his headteacher's suit,
enfolding your hands, grabbing your suitcase—*molo, molo, molo*—
the smooth grey of the airport road fracturing into dust. In praise
of his wife at home, a handwritten schedule (Day 1) and the
tablecloth tinged cobalt blue by her best water jug. In praise of
pausing at a white-washed building with a corrugated roof,
mouths shaped by God, waistcoats, hats, collars, capes in white
and red, swaying next to plant-pots weaved with sweet-paper
jewels, lingering at the jamb, listening with your skin. In praise
of the hall their fathers built, an orchestra of hands, of feet, of
thighs, of tongues, girls in blue pinafores, boys in sandy shirts,
teenagers slapping gumboots, percussive limbs conjuring
grandfathers from the mine, girls with paint-petals splashed
around their eyes, twirling orange skirts hooped with black braid,
verses in Xhosa, Zulu, Sesotho, English, Afrikaans:
Nkosi sikelel' iAfrika. In praise of Madiba
at home in Qunu where he grew, watching an armed guard pace
the barbed perimeter: *he can't see the visitor from England today*,
slipping a button-badge from Wembley '88 back inside your
pocket, walking past women who'll paint their rooms, wash their
curtains, set a price for funeral rent. In praise of Sister Clarence
delivering utensils, pans, two blankets for a boy to tuck round
his father. You sit next to her as she revs the engine, forces the
wheels over a brick, young men kick the dirt, jeer, pleased with
their game. *Inswelaboya! Where is your fur?* In praise of the stretch
of students following zigzag cracks across the fields, past a pair
of goalposts and three rusted cars, saved-for uniforms, shirts
patched with sweat, ties knotted tight to the top. In praise of
harmonies rippling along rows, soaking the soil, late-comers
scurrying past Mr Kondolo (arms folded). In praise of the boys

revising for an exam that choreographs by multiple choice, junking their desks against the wall, breaking out into the yard, filing back, stooped, stamping, slapping their shins, school ties swinging like chains and feet sweltering in Nike trainers. In praise of an orange skirt hooped with black braid, a coral-seed necklace, the rose-decorated sign from your classroom door. Unpacking you'll shudder, smile, step back. Like Proust dipping a madeleine in his tea.

Qumbu, October 2002

[Molo – isiXhosa for 'hello'; Nkosi sikelel' iAfrika – national anthem of South Africa; Madiba – clan name of Nelson Mandela; Inswelaboya – a person who has failed in Ubuntu]

II

(v.) of water, to flow with a swirling motion and a murmuring sound, to gurgle; of breath or smoke, to be emitted in a swirling stream, to eddy, also of music and the voice, to murmur

TO THE FATES

after Kathleen Jamie and Friedrich Hölderlin

in your weaving
grant me sight
just once

of it skimming the slow-flowing river
lightning-blue mantle nape to tail

in your weaving
grant me sight
just once

of it poised above the slow-flowing river
copper feathers belly to breast

in your weaving
grant me sight
just once

vertebrae leaning into corrugated bark
in the margins of the slow-flowing river

my weaving

eyes pressing into unearthed roots
on the far side of the slow-flowing river

my weaving

being where the ranger told me I should be
doing what the ranger told me I should do

my weaving
grants me sight

RETRACING

Plucking creamy-white and mocha striped jewels,
sea-silt rushing into hollows left by uncoupled valves,
our soles in the fringes *all the way up to the third groyne,*
past those wind turbines and the red buoy.

Hopping over ripples in the swash *then*
back for our flask of tea, ham sandwiches and ginger cake.
There's still room in both pockets of his burial suit,
water in our socks, sediment under our nails.

GREEN

by mudflats I thumb a second-hand guide:
black-headed gulls, what I'll say
is a curlew, and two cormorants poised
back-to-back, a heart-shaped hole between

*

late snow up by the trig
liquefies between my finger-tips
and the vent in the tarn's membrane
flashes fish I can't name yet

*

I toss ice-chips;
they skid and chime while
a merlin or sparrowhawk
freewheels into the scrub

MARKET GARDEN WAY, NATIONAL MEMORIAL ARBORETUM

And when you glide up we push at the brims
nudge the berets away from your brows

and when you lean closer for the waltz
our clasped hands tingle and trap the warmth

and when you whisk us round in circles
we grip at Pegasus stitched onto serge

and when you sink again into the Rhine
we fall, nighties ballooning like parachutes

and when we settle in the riverbed
we scatter stickleback eggs across the shingle.

Nothing is impossible reads the Renkum Stone
where we gather in black coats and stoop,

where wreaths lean and lie and leaves purl,
where the stonemason's carving persists.

SONNET

Space or place or void resting
on the surface of your mug, sheltering
underneath post-it notes curling away
and up from the wall, remembering
where, when, who, tucked inside the holes
of your watch strap, discarded for now,
leaving an answerphone message, *sorry I
can't come*, nestling round and inside
a broken egg-shell announcing, folding
into the mesh-work of a dream-catcher
absorbing what you want to forget, calling
to your friend across the street, hidden
between your pen-lid and its clip,
sending a postcard home *wish I was there.*

MOONSTONE BEACH, CA

Feet at your head, head at your feet, elbows lost
in the duvet warmed by our sleep

      I lie flat on my stomach with the binoculars

as your voice falls into the pillow
                    Is the blind up?
      and I crane my neck further

toward the window, forearms tense, fingers twisting the
   focussing wheel,
rubber eyecups rammed into my sockets
      when a humpback whale agitates the surface

I roll over, unlock the lumbar vertebrae in the curve of my back,
lever myself up on the side of your rib cage (interrupting your breath)
and dress
                    Not before pancakes.

Your voice falls into the closing door.

On the boardwalk infused with Monterey pine
I delay early-morning joggers

      watch intermittent spouts blink across the horizon
      air pushing water, mucus, CO_2 up

                    rising light

      and I catch one
           in a single round picture
                locket-sized
as it breaches, twists back into the ocean.

          White spray settles on the water

                              a dahlia in full bloom.

He doesn't know what I have seen.

Imagining you'll join me, ask for the binoculars
I track its path

                    until it leads out of sight

            then, you are behind me, hands guiding my shoulders
                    I want to press on today, reach L.A.

On the beach
a man forages among the stones
                    Look! A schiller!

His voice reaches a woman
            leaning into a washed-up Redwood bole
            who smiles when he holds up the moonstone,
            unzips her pocket for the lustre he'll bring.

MY HUSBAND AND SON CLIMB UP TO BLEA TARN

after Dorothy Wordsworth

Friday morning [16th] a refurbished swallows' nest
under the church porch—I leave a prayer
in a book by the font a silver ribbon keeps the place
—liverwort and coral-spot fungus soften
fallen branches in Stanley Ghyll and sunlight
shapes the rocks a slice beneath the water
that whispers to my instep perfumes my toes
—if they look down they might know me
re-lacing my walking boots trouser hems wet
Friday afternoon [16th] our footfall finds one pace

TAKING THE WATER

A red web is spreading
in the corner of her son's eye

and slits of the landscape peep under his closing lid:
the hawthorn he hid behind, watercress rooted in the gravel,
a grey wagtail tapping in Rag Beck

where the hem of her scarf is quickly soaked.
She tips his head back, rams his chin up,
tells him to stretch his eyes to their limit

and squeezes cotton in her fist.
A drip lengthens, pools in his socket,
catches in the lashes as his eyelid jerks

open shut open shut
and they sit and wait, under the alder
where rags (shredded from coal-streaked shirts,

wet from the Beck, sticky with pus)
once hung from the branches.

COLLECTING EVIDENCE

Lift a print from the wingbeats:
take-off, mid-flight, landing.

Use die-stone for the dints left
by the whorls and leaves and stems.

Salvage the hum of the pollen-roads
from underneath the daily commute.

And if you factor in the trajectory
of a palm-blown kiss plotted with string

from doorstep to car window,
we might have something on the sky.

PERFECT SETTING

for Barbara Hepworth

When Spring is outside, lacy with sun-leaves,
reach your fingertips round its middle,
watch the colour-shifts on its curve
and breathe through the criss-cross strings
pulled taut at its centre: a pulse.

When Spring is inside all that matters
behind the glass case is salt on bronze:
the removal man's sweat, now wiped clean.

III

(v. colloquial) *to turn upside down, overturn, capsize, to pitch or tumble head over heels*

GRAND CANYON

In memory of Georgie White Clark (1911-1992)

the Colorado wheels Georgie
in the white-water pull and push
>> and Sommona Rose cycles behind her again
>> all gawky teenage legs

on an eddy line she is flipped, grit
scrapes the inner wall of her nose
>> and Sommona Rose falls behind on the bend
>> all aching teenage legs

the churn pops her up
she grabs a sweeper
>> and sees Sommona Rose's bicycle on the tarmac
>> all tangled metal and twisted teenage legs

the currents tug at her ankles
she lets go, slips back
>> and Sommona Rose cycles behind her again
>> all gawky teenage legs

and the Colorado holds them
in the white-water pull and push

NIGHT MANOEUVRES

Her room is small, and the door must be kept shut at all times. A large sticker on the inside says so. In the corridor outside, she can hear the chatter: nurses, physios, speech therapists, the chaplain, others' visitors. She props the door open with her Jack's shell case. A nurse removes the brass tube. *It's a fire risk.* And the door eases shut. So, she presses the call button to get a glimpse—a flash of life framed by the doorway, her neighbour's great-grandson slamming his toy car into the skirting boards. *Stop wasting my time.* And the door eases shut. Tonight she's going to take direct action—she thinks that's what they call it now. *Good-old-fashioned-bloody-mindedness,* her Jack would say. She waits.

At ten o'clock her final dose of medication arrives. *Stay put.* And the door eases shut. The corridor lights dim, the strip of light under the door fades, she grips her nightie. Her Jack calls out: *it's now or never, love.* She pulls herself up by the bed rail, feels under her pillow for the knife hidden at supper time and shuffles across the room. With a hand steadier than it has been for months, she starts to unscrew the hinges of the door.

FURIES

Outside
the mistle thrush sits tall on his perch
and rehearses his song in dread of the fieldfares
that raid the garden's dwindling stores.

Inside the white room
she accepts a bunch of unseasonal flowers;
he stands with his thumb down a pinstripe seam

and when he's gone
she pounds her fists until the grout clogs with red
and she's hoisted by her armpits, slung on the bed

where she watches them at work,
in Technicolor, across her lids,
sprinkling salt in his tea,
cutting paper dolls
in the folds of *The Times*.

Outside
heronries nest as many as ten pairs
while a fluffed teal splashes
and a shelduck tosses his emerald head.

Inside the white room
she accepts a bunch of unseasonal flowers;
he stands with his thumb down a pinstripe seam

and when he's gone
she pounds her fists until the grout clogs with red
and she's hoisted by her armpits, slung on the bed

where she watches them at work,
in Technicolor, across her lids,
pinching his doughy
calves until he cramps

under Irish linen sheets.

Outside
leaves mesh green through brown moss
and hazel catkins expand;
snowdrops shine.

Inside the white room
she accepts a bunch of unseasonal flowers;
he stands with his thumb down a pinstripe seam

and when he's gone

DEAD RINGER

Waiting at the lights he spots
a woman leaning against
the wall of the Hope and Anchor.
She grabs at the air. Misses.
Her shoulder smacks concrete slabs.

She levers herself up from the dog-ends,
presses her spine into the bricks
disc by disc by disc. The string
of a storybook-balloon seems to tug
at her crown; she is tall.

Three undone-buttons lay bare
her collarbone and he pictures
the blood-red vascular spiders
circulating under her skin.
Her eyes will be bilirubin yellow.

And she'll be wearing
the same boozy perfume
that once seeped
from the bedsheets as he
tucked them in around his wife.

The flatbed in front pulls away.

HIGH DEPENDENCY

He waits and scratches along the purple ripple stretching
from thenar to wrist, where the chainsaw peeled his skin
and exposed his carpal bones to the leaves of an oak.

He waves and the corridor light comes back on.
Visiting finished hours ago and nurses cocooned
in their stations don't know he's there. He paces.

When the door yawns open, he expects a cousin
with a mouthful of braces, fringe flicked, frozen
and claggy with hairspray. He sees a mother.

The cafeteria is closed. In the light of a vending machine,
you show him the Polaroid and explain the tubes.
He buys you a Mars bar; you don't ask if he's clean.

HARWICH

At the end of Ha'penny Pier
ground frost takes his rear tyre.
The left pedal gouges the timber
and a flexed leg saves him;
the key jabs into his hip bone.
Across the estuary,
cirrus clouds drag comet-tails
and tangle with the container crane
unloading *Evelyn Maersk,*
her saxe-blue hull dimmed by oil—
Ken and *Barbie,* in their thousands,
arriving from China via Malaysia,
Singapore, Gibraltar, Algeciras,
hands linked behind cellophane.
He stamps the padlock
through the deck planks
and marks the drop
with a wreath of splinters.

HAIRCUTS

You called to tell me, and I came in time
to see her pushed along the corridor, curls shaved.
At three, she lost her grasp on how to walk
and they needed to work on the cells crowding
inside her head (disorganised, oversized, variable),
taking up space. On high stools we ate breakfast
from polystyrene capsules, watched the street.

Today, you call to tell me about your final cut of the day,
a man whose *neck hair needed a good trim*, how he saw her
in the mirror, a teenager with curls by your shoulder.

Her breath tickled your neck: *tell her*
her daughter's not expected yet.
On a high stool I eat breakfast
from a polystyrene capsule, watch the street.

PERCHING AT THE BACK OF A RIB

where damselflies frisk the prow
under the bridge

we jerk the strap tight
across your life-vest
and shoulder to shoulder
squeeze in for a photo

mum and dad and son
mama and baba

fingers picking
at his crusted cheeks
at the salt weighing on his lashes
worrying at his wet hoodie

in the channel
where the sky presses down

mama, baba, djalë
mum, dad, son

ARAPUCA

A pyramid of tied sticks hidden
where he used to pass—under
the motorway bridge, by the van
handing out blankets, hot soup.

The cage fell, penned him in
for long days tarmacking drives
of semis on the edge of town.
His weight barely triggered it.

A heavy-bellied man took the stand,
said he'd provided a place to live:
a fair exchange for labour.
He couldn't explain the horse-box
with three others, their bruised ribs.

SKEGNESS WAKE

Graffiti on the carcass shouts: MANS FAULT
but the woman next to me isn't so sure.

A burgundy membrane drapes from its insides
and a chainsaw settles in the sand

where we toy with the flapping cordon, study
the squid scars on the box-shaped head,

an amputated jawbone and conical teeth.
She quizzes the pathologist

leaning on a 4x4, clipboard jammed
against his hip. He can't answer yet

and walks into the sea,
green chest-waders up to his armpits.

Salt water rinses the blood-spatter
from his face and a Jack Russell sniffs

at fluids pooling beneath the flukes.
An oily odour is binding to the fibres of the gloves

I post later in the bin by Terry's Fish 'N' Chips.
They say there are two more at Gibraltar Point

so I join the column drawn there and back,
calves burning in the back-slide of the shingle.

STOPPER ON THE POACHER LINE

leaving the platform   buddleia, warehouses, vandal fences,
mildewed swing-seats in back gardens, cerise plastic sheeting (hooked on
dormant branches) flicking up and back like flamenco skirts
    Fen-water gathering in ditches   and near Great Hale Eau three
cormorants displaying their wings to a sord of mallard napping on the bank,
heads tucked in

                    caravans, a shipping container: off-grid
    breaking into fields bordering the Trent, fallstreaks from the clouds
nudge the grass; two pheasants lurch up in a dash for fresh cover—racing,
tails resisting air   cerise plastic sheeting (hooked on dormant branches)
flicking up and back like flamenco skirts, mildewed swing-seats in back
gardens, vandal fences, warehouses, buddleia   arriving at the platform

sand lodged in the tread of my boots, stomach still tight from the spectacle:
indentations of flukes and whale tissue packed in polystyrene for the archive

BRANCASTER BEACH

An early wave of cars reaches the saltmarsh road,
breaking for spaces that lap at the boardwalk.
Car boots spill Labradors, spades, windbreaks,
sausage rolls, wet-suits itchy with yesterday's sand

onto the footpath by fairway and green—hostages
of our warming sea. At the kiosk piles of buckets
stretch up to the wrists of a woman in the queue.
Her cheeks accept a gentle westerly, her lips

smart at the polystyrene-tea and a gossamer life
flutters in her womb. In the dunes kite-string
shadows dart across reddening backs and SS Vina,
gnawed by salt, rises in the mudflats at low tide.

A seal, sun blistering its distended belly, knocks against the hull.

VARIATIONS ON A THEME, 1943

This piece of shrapnel
its tip stained sky

from passing through, chipping the lens

snags on my palm
haunts the canvas
bends light over concentric ridges
each ray refracts slightly more

the lantern turned, rasped
until one perfect beam
every five seconds

> *Richard Grenfell, 62, light keeper of The Solent*
> *salt and smoke clotting in his throat.*

This piece of shrapnel
its tip stained sky

from passing through, chipping the lens

sinks into my palm
haunts the canvas
bends light over concentric ridges
each ray refracts slightly more

the lantern turned, rasped
until one perfect beam
every five seconds

> *William Jones, 50, light keeper of The Solent*
> *salt and smoke clotting in his throat.*

This piece of shrapnel
its tip stained sky

from passing through, chipping the lens

settles in my palm
haunts the canvas
bends light over concentric ridges
each ray refracts slightly more

the lantern turned, rasped
until one perfect beam
every five seconds

> *Charles Tompkins, 47, light keeper of the Solent*
> *salt and smoke clotting in his throat.*

SOUTH BANK CATCH-UP

Just metres away an oily armour-piercing shell
(a sprat palpitating in its fuse pocket) is towed out past Essex,
    detonated.

You order Bellinis
named after the artist

and perhaps the colour
mixed for St. Christopher's robe as he crossed the water

eyes rolled up at the Child riding his shoulder
brown hair clamped in two fists.

A kidney-bean bulges
in the blood vessel behind your fringe.

You only tell us about your three,
how you let them run naked down to the stream at the bottom
    of the fields.

NICU

I

buzzed in at nine

through the porthole
a boy with wrinkle-sag
knees shelters his fingers
in the antiseptic furrows
of your cupped palm;
from your perch
on next door's vacant
stool, you anticipate
back spasms

four hours later
litmus paper stutters
in your fingers—*is pink
red?* and your milk tubes
down into his stomach

now a sodden nappy snags
on the cannula impaled
in his gauzy vein; cotton
wool and titanium ointment
jumble around his legs

at bedtime
your lullaby keeps time
with his heart's
beep

buzzed out at nine

II

It's just in case.
A Polaroid, 2" by 3½":

> tangles of tubes and wires snake to a body frozen
> in the position of his foetal scan
> air pushes down the endotracheal tube and he breathes
> the right pattern.

Tuck him under your pillow.